Laughing with Lutherans

Highlights from 20 years
of *The Lutheran*'s "Light side"

Ed Fischer

Edited by Julie B. Sev

D0289060

Laughing with Lutherans

Highlights from 20 Years of *The Lutheran*'s "Light side"

Skandisk, Inc.
6667 West Old Shakopee Road
Suite 109
Bloomington, Minnesota 55438
www.skandisk.com

ISBN 10: 1-57534-075-5
ISBN 13: 978-1-57534-075-3

Library of Congress Control Number: 2008940133

Cover design and spot illustrations by Kirsten Sevig

Printed in the United States of America

Table of Contents

Introduction 4

Pastors and their families 6

Oops: bulletin and other bloopers 22

Kids say the wisest things 46

Music, worship and such 74

Lutheran this and that 84

Through the seasons: Advent through Pentecost 95

Good answers 122

What's so funny about weddings and funerals? .. 126

Stewardship and other money matters 132

Congregational life 136

When *The Lutheran* makes the "Light side"...... 139

Study guide 143

Dedicated to all the readers of *The Lutheran* who have over the years observed and laughed about all the funny things that happen at church. Thank you for taking time to write them down and send them in so others could enjoy these moments.

In memory of Alfred and Olive Sevig, who instilled in me a need to be part of a faith community, and who passed along a sense of humor gene that keeps me (somewhat) sane and grounded.

Special thanks to the cartoonists and illustrators whose work appears on the pages of this book:

Cartoonists:

Francis H. Brummer   Gruber and Denton   Dik LaPine
Martha Campbell   David W. Harbaugh   Jean Sorensen
Dave Drumm   Norman Jung   Bob Vojtko
Dennis Fletcher

Illustrators: Kirsten Sevig and Ed Fischer
Typesetting and design: Lisa Hamnes and Else Sevig

Introduction

"It's the most-read page in the magazine," I tell people. At least that's what one survey of our readers confirmed. The "Light side" page of *The Lutheran* magazine has for 20 years given Lutherans of the Evangelical Lutheran Church in America a dose of much-needed levity.

On any given day, I receive in my work mailbox a church bulletin with a blooper circled, or an e-mail recounting the cute (and often profound) observation of a child or grandchild. Many of them work their way into the magazine, enabling others throughout the church to enjoy the moment these folks observed or experienced.

It is a gift, isn't it, this ability to laugh at ourselves? Especially in a church setting? In the church and into all corners of our secular world, there is plenty of fodder for disagreement. But on this one little page each month there is something that brings us together because we can see ourselves there. These true stories, often built on a human foible, make us smile—maybe even laugh.

The selections on these pages have been culled from 20 years of "Light side" pages. They are the "best of," gathered here for your enjoyment. And they're paired with the other gift we offer each month: cartoons from some of *The Lutheran*'s favorite cartoonists.

Delight in these selections and cartoons. And while Allen Funt warned viewers to beware of that "Candid Camera," I say keep your candid camera running. Observe, take note, smile, laugh, remember and send your stories to *The Lutheran*. Pay attention when a voice within you (or near you) says, "That could make the 'Light side.' " After all, the page is depending on you.

In gratefulness,
Julie B. Sevig
"Light side" editor

The Lutheran magazine, 8765 W. Higgins Rd., Chicago, IL 60631
julie.sevig@thelutheran.org

Pastors and their families

"So, we have a choice... to continue to present the image of a perfect pastor and spouse team... or to allow the children to start attending church."

While bringing communion to a member at a residential care facility, I was greeted by one of the nursing staff who recognized me as the pastor of the congregation where she'd recently brought some residents to worship. She remarked, "Pastor, you look much different in your clothes!"

David D. Olson
Sandpoint, ID

My pastor husband likes to sit with the family during congregational hymns, but on Easter Sunday the church was so full he sat in the big chair in the sanctuary. Our perplexed 3-year-old daughter whispered, "Is Daddy having a time-out?"

Pam Hulstrand
Portland, ND

In the family picture taken for our sons' confirmation my husband wore his black suit and clerical collar. I displayed that photo beside my bed when hospitalized. An employee asked why we photographed the boys with the family priest. Mischievously, I was tempted to say, "That's the boys' father," and leave it at that.

Karen Swanson
Dayton, IA

The newsletter of Faith Lutheran Church, Valders, Wisconsin, included the following note:

Pastor Peters and Marlene will be on vacation May 19-26. If pastoral scare is needed—call Pastor Mark.

Hildegarde Honold
Valders, WI

Instructions to sound system operators posted at Bethesda Lutheran Church, Eugene, Oregon, read:

"Remember both pastors have their own mikes. If the pastor sounds funny, send an usher to get him a new battery. That will be the problem 90 percent of the time."

Judy L. Jernberg
Eugene, OR

After a retired pastor's wife fainted at church and 911 was called, a paramedic asked her these questions: "What's your name?" "Where are you?" and, "What day is it?" to which she answered, "The Third Sunday in Advent." Of course, it was.

Howard D. Wagner
Moorhead, MN

Proclaiming PK

My first Sunday at Zion Lutheran Church, Madison, Wisconsin, was going well as I stumbled through the particulars of a new place. When I was five minutes into the sermon, my 3-year-old came up front and tugged on my pants leg. I took a break and asked, "Jake, is there something you need help with?" His response: "We're at a new church, Daddy. You've gotta tell them about that day Jesus died and then God brought him back on Sunday. They may not know that one."

Pat Siegler
Madison, WI

**Pastor Jim's sons avoid punishment with the
"distract him with a sermon illustration" technique.**

11

My husband asked during the children's sermon on Christmas Eve, "What is coming?" He received a full range of answers—Santa, presents, Grandma, Rudolf. Finally, he called on our 5-year-old daughter who was excitedly waving her hand, confident she had the answer he was looking for. She proudly declared, "Hanukkah!"

Linda J. Conway
Princeton, NJ

Church council members at Grace Lutheran Church, Corvallis, Oregon, read the back of their ballots, which had been made by cutting up old Lenten bulletins. On the pastor's ballot was "Truly, I say to you, one of you will betray me..." And on the ballot of the incumbent chair, "Is it I?"

E.H. Kindschuh & Hal Dick
Corvallis, OR

Good to the last decade

Shortly after our marriage in 1938 when my wife and I moved into the parsonage of Bethany Lutheran Church in Central Bridge, New York, we found the kitchen table over-flowing with the gift of groceries. Among the goodies was a one-pound can of coffee, which for some reason was put away and forgotten.

On the eve of our 50th wedding anniversary we opened the can of Beechnut vacuum-packed coffee and on the morning of our anniversary we drank the half-century old coffee for breakfast. Those were the best cups of coffee we'd had in a long time. Thanks to someone, perhaps now long gone from this world, whose thoughtful, loving gift brought joy to our family 50 years later!

David C. Gaise
Toms River, NJ

"I've changed my mind about wanting weekly feedback on my sermons."

© Dennis Fletcher

FLETCHER

Last week one of my confirmation students wrote this sermon note, "The sermon was about the 6th Commandment which is adultery and the pastor's trip to California."

Diane Faust
Obelisk, PA

I winced as I reviewed the sermon notes at First Lutheran Church of Crystal, Brooklyn Park, Minnesota, on what part of the service the ninth graders found meaningful. One boy said it was the sermon: "The microphone went out and I couldn't hear very well."

Dale E. Howard
Brooklyn Park, MN

Sunday mornings I would get up early to review my sermon and prepare for worship. When my son, Jeremy, was 5, he wandered into my study one Sunday and asked what I was doing. When I told him I was practicing my sermon, he asked if he could listen. I proceeded to read through it as Jeremy listened attentively. When I finished he asked, "Is that it?" "Yes," I replied, "What did you think of it?" Without hesitation he answered, "Long enough."

John Gugel
Muskego, WI

"And to all you late arrivals... Anyone can get to church on time if he tries hard enough."

As the new pastor's stole was presented during a recent ordination service, the worship booklet reprinted Matthew 11:20-30 to be read:

"Take my yolk upon you... For my yolk is easy, and my burden is light." Some of us found it fitting that this passage was read after the laying on of "hens."

Ron Luckey
Lexington, KY

I recently retired from parish ministry. Due to my grandchild's baptism, I had my alb [vestment] hanging in the car. When my 7-year-old grandson, Sean, saw my car, he said, "Grandpa, I see you didn't have to turn in your uniform."

Jim Hunter
Gresham, OR

In the spirit of the Scandinavian heritage of Our Savior Lutheran Church, Glen Head, New York, I have said "takk" to our Korean-American choir director after each rehearsal. After 10 years I assumed he knew what I meant. Recently he asked what that meant and I said, "Thanks." "Oh, good," he said. "In Korean 'tak' means 'chicken.'"

Paul T. Johnson
Glen Head, NY

© Jean Sorensen

"About the charity auction — does 'Dinner with the Pastor' include a sermon? People are asking."

From a letter to members of Bethel Lutheran Church, Santa Maria, California:

"Pastor T. has recently completed 35 years of service since his ordination. We are privileged to have this millstone occur during his service at Bethel."

Donovan Lee
Cedar Ridge, CA

Oops: bulletin and other bloopers

"Our secretary doesn't consider them typos.
She prefers to think of them as her word processor
speaking in an unknown font."

The funeral service computer template at St. Mark Lutheran Church, Van Wert, Ohio, includes the name of the deceased at appropriate places in the liturgy and prayers. A funeral for a woman named Edna followed a funeral for a woman named Mary. The secretary used the search-and-replace function to substitute "Edna" for "Mary." But to the pastor's chagrin, when the congregation was invited to confess the Apostles' Creed, he saw the worship folder read, "Born of the Virgin Edna."

Mike Sherer
Findlay, OH

In Christ United Lutheran Church,
Gordon, Pennsylvania, bulletin:

"CULC annual picnic at St. John's Grove.
Bring lawn chairs to sin on."

Martha Bingaman
Gordon, PA

In the Immanuel Lutheran Church,
Irwin, Pennsylvania, bulletin:

"[Christmas] decorating party for church
Sunday at 2 p.m. Bring saw to cut trees and
willing hands."

A.P. Brannick
North Huntingdon, PA

This notice was left on the door for the Hispanic custodian of St. Matthew Lutheran Church, North Hollywood, California:

Ken Koonce
Los Angeles, CA

In the Lutheran Church of the Servant,
Santa Fe, New Mexico, bulletin:

"Senior citizen recycling will begin at the
three senior citizen centers in Santa Fe next
Saturday."

Helen Wagner
Santa Fe, NM

From the minutes of the retirees group of
St. Paul Lutheran Church, York, Pennsylvania:

"After eating, Neil thanked the committee for
making soup which consisted of Esther S.,
Dorothy S. and Beulah H."

Thelma Drayer
York, PA

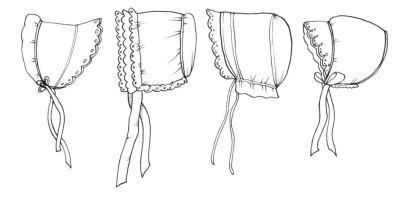

From the minutes of the ecclesiastical arts committee, St. Paul Lutheran Church, Littlestown, Pennsylvania:

"Baptismal bonnets on hand are: 3 girls, 1 boy. There are 4 boys in the process of being made."

R. Zepp
Littlestown, PA

"Who said Hallelujah?"

In the Rocky Mountain Synod Newsletter:

"Musician wanted: Avondale Lutheran Church is looking for a pianist for Sunday morning worship services at 9 and 10:30 a.m. Must know how to play the piano in Spanish."

Florence Dirks
Longmont, CO

In the Peace Lutheran Church,
Manhattan, Kansas, bulletin:

"Before the lecture he will be discussing his personal faith struggle in suffering at a potluck supper."

Dave MacFarland
Manhattan, KS

The building/operations committee report in the Bethel Lutheran Church, Seattle, Washington, newsletter said:

"Special thanks to Arnie E. for washing widows."

Jane L. Asmann
Bothell, WA

In the Grace Lutheran Church,
Pittsburgh, Pennsylvania, bulletin:

"The Grace Lutheran Church Women are planning an 'English Tea Party,' inviting the women of area Lutheran churches. All women are asked to wear hats and gloves; no slacks, please."

James McKee
Library, PA

Stay away from the 9:30 service

In the Benton-Harbor-St. Joseph, Michigan, *Herald-Palladium:*

"Saron Lutheran Church of St. Joseph will dedicate four works of art in memory of eight persons who have died over the past several years at the conclusion of the 9:30 a.m. worship service."

Gloria Currie
Granger, IN

In the Mount Zion Evangelical Lutheran Church, Pittsburgh, Pennsylvania, bulletin:

"We will have a reception after the service. Libby H. is coordinating persons to bake cakes and kitchen workers. Please volunteer today."

Eva Cutenese
Pittsburgh, PA

At Our Lord Lutheran Church, Oklahoma City, Oklahoma, after repair of the drinking fountain which had long suffered with poor water pressure, this sign was placed above it:

"If thou presseth too hard upon the button, thou shalt be reminded of thy baptism."

James Collings
Oklahoma City, OK

Sign in Pennsylvania church cemetery:

"Persons are prohibited from picking flowers from any but their own graves."

Christine Lyszczak
Trenton, NJ

And this mailing label from—of all places—the U.S. Department of Education, who should know the proper spelling:

"Attention Principle,
Atonement Lutheran School"

Rick Mueller
Florissant, MO

Vow removal

The newsletter from Grace Lutheran Church, Rochester, Pennsylvania, described a Valentine's Day service that would include renewal of vows for couples:

"...those married 70 years or more will come forward; those who have been married 50 years or more will come forward; then all married couples who wish to have their marriage vows removed may follow."

Joan Enke
Rochester, PA

"We're probably the only church newsletter that consistently has to go to a second printing."

On the Sunday before Valentine's Day the bulletin contained the following twist on the words of institution:

"In the nighty in which he was betrayed, our Lord Jesus took bread ..." A new member joining that day asked me if this was "the romantic version."

Julie Bergdahl
Plattsburgh, NY

Who knows how the senior citizens at Lutheran Church of the Atonement, Florissant, Missouri, will fare at their August tour of Missouri wineries? A notation in early publicity said: "arraignments to follow."

Rick Mueller
Florissant, MO

The Mount Zion Lutheran Church, LaGrange, Indiana, bulletin noted:

"There will not be a Week of Prayer for Unity Service next Sunday due to schedule conflicts for five of the six congregations involved."

William Griffith
Sturgis, MI

St. Peter Evangelical Lutheran Church, Washington, D.C., newsletter:

Ash Wednesday [Service]: Worship with Imposition of Ushers, 7:30 p.m.

Ida Mae Donley
Brentwood, MD

As a teacher of religion at Carthage College, Kenosha, Wisconsin, term papers enlighten me. One student confided, "As I grew up, I learned that Jesus suffered and died for us so we can have a chance to live a sinful life."

But more entertaining are the results of spell-check corrections, such as: I learned that Jesus went to Gerasene to heal the democrats (demoniacs?) and that Jesus' body was taken from the cross by Joseph of Aromatherapy.

Ross Henry Larson
Kenosha, WI

"Would you like some busy work?"

Zion Lutheran Church, Garretson,
South Dakota, bulletin:

"7:30 Lenten Service. The final Lenten Service
theme is 'Why Doesn't God Do Something?'
with Pastor Meidinger."

Anonymous
Garretson, SD

I was surprised when a pastor at a church I
was visiting announced a meeting of "The
Ladies of the Evening Circle." Apparently he
was differentiating it from the morning and
afternoon circles.

Ruth Nicholson
West Columbia, SC

Speedy results

From the Immanuel Lutheran Church, San Jose, California, *Evangel*, announcing a fundraiser for the benefit floor project:

"So plan now to eat breakfast at the church on Easter, make a contribution for your breakfast and then see your results on the floor."

Dean Rystad
San Jose, CA

"The church secretary just left for a job less stressful. She joined the Marines."

At a 1998 Delaware-Maryland Synod assembly worship service, Bishop George Mocko sent worshipers off with these words:

"May the God of Abraham and Sarah call you to New Jersey." When the snickers subsided he corrected himself, "... call you to new journeys in faith."

Sandra Carlson Alexis
Leitersburg, MD

From the Perley [Minnesota] Lutheran Parish bulletin:

"Next weekend 11 Luther Leaguers plus two chaperones will be in St. Cloud for the Synod Youth Fathering."

David Hunstad
Moorhead, MN

© Martha F. Campbell

"Math has never been one of the pastor's strong points."

From the newsletter of St. Mark Lutheran Church,
Springfield, Virginia:

"Tom B. will address Lenten fasts and the
practical points of fasting and Linda R. will
bring the doughnuts."

Tom Berkey
Burke, VA

Council minutes from Christ the King Lutheran Church,
Dodge City, Kansas:

"Parish Education: Rally Day went well with
the horses being a big hit. Pastor John has
three in his new member class."

Arlyce Gerdes
Dodge City, KS

Kids say the wisest things

**"We had an Old Testament skit today.
Bucky Sims was the Hittite and I was the Hittee."**

My 3-year-old grandson was having problems at nursery school with a little girl who pinched and punched him. His dad advised him to tell her it wasn't nice. When it happened again his mom asked if he did what dad told him to do. "No," he responded, "But I took care of it. I asked God to turn her into a rabbit."

William E. Smith
Crouse, NC

When I asked my youngest nephew, Joshua, if he would be in church that coming Sunday, he replied: "Oh, yes. Because my brother is going to be the pilot light."

Greg Moe
Moorland, IA

One of our 5-year-olds recently asked his mom and dad on the way home from worship, "Why does pastor always read from St. Paul but never from St. Louis?"

Dewey Wisner
St. Charles, MO

Two of our granddaughters visited us recently. Although they normally do not attend a worship service, we took them with us to church. They knelt with us at the communion rail, and the pastor placed his hand on each small head and blessed them.

Recounting the experience the next day to their mother, the 8-year-old said, "They passed out wine and crackers. We didn't get any, but he told me a secret."

Dean Myers
White Plains, NY

My 5-year-old son was seated on the sofa next to my wife. Out of the blue he asked, "Mommy, how do you make love?" His mother swallowed hard and asked, "What do you mean?" He then responded by gesturing with his little hand in an attempt to make the American Sign Language abbreviation for "I love you," which consists of thumb and index finger up, middle fingers down and pinkie up. Having thus made "love," his mother was quite relieved.

John Hazel Jr.
White Haven, PA

"My Dad just told me the facts of life, and I can't believe you'd create such a weird system."

Young people from St. Andrew Lutheran Church, Lake Worth, Florida, which still has worship services in both English and Finnish, were recently on a youth trip to the Florida Keys. While in a diving shop the equipment manager asked the group, "How many fins?" One of the girls answered, "We all are."

Sharon Arnold
West Palm Beach, FL

Upon being introduced to the pastor and told he is "the minister in charge of this church," one of the preschoolers at St. Luke Lutheran Church, Farmingdale, New York, piped up, "NO-o-o....God's in charge."

Terri Shizume
Farmingdale, NY

Careful, Moses

The director of music at Our Redeemer Lutheran Church, Garden Grove, California, was telling the cherub choir the story behind "Moses, You Aren't Listening!" She told about Moses seeing the burning bush and walking toward it and asked "Do you know what happened next?" Allison, 6, offered, "Stop, drop and roll?"

Mellie Moreland
Mission Viejo, CA

Six-year-old Julie was sitting in the narthex of Our Saviour Lutheran Church, Fond du Lac, Wisconsin, before the Wednesday evening Lenten service. As the pastor greeted her, she asked, "Are we having a half service or a full service tonight?" Wondering what she meant, he said, "We're going to sing and pray, read from the Bible and have a sermon. Is that a half service or a full service?" "Are we having communion?" she asked. "Not tonight," the pastor replied. "Then it's a half service," Julie answered. "Such theological acumen at a young age!" the pastor observed.

Gerald V. Goodrich
Oconomowoc, WI

A 4-year-old greeted me after worship during this year's Olympics by saying, "Hi Pastor. I see the cross around your neck is silver. You must be in second place."

Paul M. Youngdahl
Minneapolis, MN

Recently some yard-less friends asked if they could bury their deceased cat in our yard. After they had gone, I invited my 8-year-old daughter to join me as we placed a cross on the grave. "Daddy, was that cat a Lutheran?" she asked. "I don't know," I answered. After a few minutes of pondering she responded, "I know, Daddy, it probably was Catlick!"

Richard S. Hinger
Springfield, OH

Three-year-old Brett, beginning to add petitions to his memorized prayers, one evening surprised his parents by thanking God for toilet paper. Since there was no lack of toilet tissue in the house, his mom reminded him to pray for something important. "Toilet paper is important," Brett said. Unable to refute that fact, Brett's parents listened to several evening prayers thanking God for that all-important toilet paper.

Margaret Perry
Marietta, GA

When my son was a preschooler we passed by a cat that had been killed by a car. My son became quite upset, and I reassured him that Jesus would come and take the cat to heaven. This seemed to calm him down. Days later when for the third time we passed the rather sad remains, my son became quite indignant, "I sure wish Jesus would come and get that darn cat."

Sandra Kovacevic
Santa Maria, CA

Perhaps this is the result of the heritage represented in our congregation. When a first grader was asked how she likes school she responded, "It's OK, but every morning we have to say 'The pledge of Norwegians.' "

Greg VanDunk
Dayton, OH

"And this is good-bye, God. We're moving in the morning."

A couple in our congregation had their visiting grandson, Henry, then 5, hold the bucket for empty plastic communion cups while they served communion. The next morning Henry said to his grandma: "Next time I'll serve the drinks and you can do the trash."

Cheryl Geller
Minot, ND

When a young girl accompanied her grandparents to the altar rail at Augustana Lutheran Church, Boone, Iowa, and heard the communion assistant say "This is the blood of Christ shed for you," she looked up and said, "You're kidding, right?"

David Abram
Urbanville, IA

My kindergarten-aged grandson is an avid baseball fan. His little friend, who is Roman Catholic, invited him to have lunch. My grandson informed his mother that they let him say his table prayer before they said theirs. "You know, Mom," he said, "it's a lot like ours only they have more hand signals."

Mildred E. Jones
Morrisonville, WI

As Ken Hovland, pastor of Rejoice Lutheran Church, Coppell, Texas, raised the chalice during the communion liturgy my 4-year-old grandson, James Kunkel, turned to his dad and asked "Daddy, did he win the trophy?"

Priscilla Kunkel
Manhattan, KS

One of the boys in my second grade Sunday school class missed several weeks. His mother said he'd had strep throat. When he returned I told him I was glad he was over his illness. He replied, "I didn't have strep. I had hockey."

Elizabeth Husberg
West St. Paul, MN

Mrs. McElroy was teaching the Sunday school fifth-graders about being good stewards of what God has given us. "Next week I want you to bring something that you have too much of," she told them. A voice from the back asked, "Can I bring my little sister?"

Paul M. Strom
Menominee, MI

Where's Jesus?

When my 3-year-old asks where Jesus lives
I reply, "He lives in your heart." One day
during lunch I was especially tickled when my
son swallowed a bit of food and asked with a
concerned look, "Do you think that hit Jesus
on the way down?"

Rosie Gonzalez
Logansport, IN

During a long confirmation service at Bethel
Lutheran Church, Little Falls, Minnesota, our
sports-minded 3-year-old leaned over and
whispered loudly, "This is sure going into
overtime!"

Mary Jane Wolters
Little Falls, MN

"Too late. I already asked God to make my team win."

Several years ago when I was one of two female pastors serving St. James Evangelical Lutheran, Pitman, New Jersey, the congregation observed the 50th ordination of its former pastor, a man. This came as a shock to a 6-year-old girl who remarked to her mother, "Can a man be a pastor?"

Carol Brighton
Ramsey, NJ

Too new to be old...

Dale's mother asked: "Do you know who Jesus is?" The 4-year-old said, "Sure, the baby Jesus in the crib." "Yes," she said, "but he grew to become a boy and then a man." He replied, "Oh no, Mama. I don't think so. He was just born at Christmas."

Ethelyn Berns
Monona, IA

I left my 11-year-old son home one evening while I went to my older daughter's school concert. He called me five times while I was driving home, frightened because a thunderstorm was brewing. When I got home I sat in bed with him and snuggled. He said, "Mom, I think after God got done making thunder and lightning, that's when he decided he needed to make mamas."

Paige Fiedler
Johnston, IA

I must admit that our family's summer church attendance isn't so regular. My 3-year-old daughter Kim said one day as we drove by our church, Grace Lutheran in Fairmont, West Virginia, "Hey, there's the church we don't go to."

Andrew Gamber
Fairmont, WV

"I didn't say my prayers,
but I e-mailed God earlier."

To keep my younger son quiet in church, I supply him with a pencil and paper and hope he's paying attention. One Sunday the service was especially long with extra hymns and a baptism. After lunch the boys went out into the back yard to play. After a while I heard water coming from the bathroom. Investigating, I saw my son standing by the sink clutching a large grasshopper in one hand and small bar of soap in the other. He held it under the water and said, "I baptize you in the name of the Father, Son and the Holy Soap." He had been paying attention!

Lynn L. Hicks
Harrah, OK

Our grandson watched with interest as our pastor incorporated the use of a yo-yo into the children's sermon. The following week I asked Max what he might want to be when he grows up: fireman, policeman.... "How about a pastor?" I asked. "Oh, no," he said. "I don't know how to work a yo-yo."

Ed & Judy Lictenhagen
Flat Rock, NC

During a worship skit at Bethany Lutheran Church, Elmira, New York, Jim, who was playing God, hid in the sacristy with a microphone. Then we heard his booming voice: "Adam, Eve, come here. I want you." A mother sitting with her 5-year-old daughter kept murmuring. "I know that voice. I know that voice." Her daughter responded, "Well, you should! It's God."

Judy Blair
Elmira, NY

Residing in a predominately Norwegian community, my brother, at a very young age, came home from Sunday School and inquired, "Who is Ole Ghost?"

David Smedal
Stoughton, WI

The color purple

I don't normally wear shorts anymore due to all the noticeable veins on my legs. But last summer while taking care of our grandchildren in Pipestone, Minnesota, I was wearing shorts when Aubrey Anna, who was lying on her tummy at my feet, said, "Grandy, I just love your legs" "You do?" I asked. "Why?" "Because," she answered, "purple is my second favorite color."

Andrea Nelson
Wittenberg, WI

"The best part was when they passed the money around—I got two quarters."

When my 4-year-old granddaughter shared her new Bible storybook with me, she animatedly told me the story of Adam and Eve, ending with "Then they ate the apple, and God put them on time-out!"

Bonnie Ender
West Salem, WI

My friend Debbie Howard was teaching her young daughter the Lord's Prayer when Kayla found a special way to personalize it: "Our Father who art in heaven, Howard be thy name..."

Karen Southward
Pickerington, OH

My grandson, Scott, 14, who loves cars, was sitting beside me in church. The pastor's sermon was about praying for others. He asked us to tell the person beside us our greatest need. Scott turned to me and said, "I need a Camaro."

N. Earl Townsend
Greensboro, NC

Vain in Maine...

Some friends were on vacation in Maine, and while watching fireworks heard their small son say, "Oh, God!" The father quickly cautioned his son, "Please don't speak the Lord's name in vain." The boy nodded but obviously misheard, because he asked quietly, "Is it OK if I speak his name back in Minnesota?"

Tom Kovach
Park Rapids, MN

Shhhh

My husband and I have been trying to encourage our 3-year-old to stay in his bed through the night. We have told him that even though Mommy and Daddy aren't always with him, Jesus is. Recently my son came into our bedroom, too early as usual. I told him to go back to bed, and he said he couldn't: "Jesus is sleeping in there and I don't want to wake him."

Koren Scott
South Bend, IN

Music, worship and such

"I'd like to inform the new members that we have a Ms. Sharp and a Mr. Flat in our choir, so don't be alarmed."

To avoid so much standing during the service, our worship and music committee decided the congregation would sit during the sermon hymn. The first week the pastor announced that we would all remain seated for the sermon hymn, laughter and confusion followed when he sat down and the organist struck up the hymn, "Stand Up, Stand Up for Jesus."

L. Bartelson
Fresno, CA

The Maundy Thursday bulletin at St. Peter Evangelical Lutheran Church, Baldwin, New York, listed as the choir anthem: "Surely, He Hath Borne Our Briefs."

E. Phillip Sebastian
Baldwin, NY

"Just because the pastor doesn't use notes,
doesn't mean the choir shouldn't!"

The worship/music committee at St. John Lutheran Church, Westville, New Jersey, smiled when it reviewed the music director's suggestion for hymns at a communion service. "Let Us Break Bread Together on Our Knees" was followed by "O Happy Day When We Shall Stand."

Paul Hirth
Westville, NJ

One night our regular organist, Grace, was late to our Search Bible Study, which usually opens with a hymn. A reluctant replacement was laboring through the first verse until Grace arrived. Someone quipped, "Ah, saved by Grace."

James A. Darchuk
Libby, MT

At a worship service celebrating the beginning of the ELCA, the words printed in the bulletin for "A Mighty Fortress" brought new meaning to Martin Luther's admonition to sin boldly: "Let goods and kindred go, this moral life also..."

Nan Schroeder
Cedar Rapids, IA

Choir members at Underwood [Iowa] Lutheran Church inserted ribbon bookmarkers in our hymnals with a hot glue gun. A soprano picked up one, putting her hand on the still warm glue spot. "Wow! That's almost too hot to handle," she exclaimed. "Well that's the first time that's been said of the Lutheran Book of Worship," said another member.

Ann Jeanette Lee
Neola, IA

The moment when lay reader Larry realizes that the Hebrew Scripture is actually in Hebrew!

A recent tornado-like storm hit Rummel, Pennsylvania. The steeple at Grace Lutheran Church was toppled. As parishioners arrived for the service the next Sunday they were surprised to learn that the entrance hymn (selected weeks before) was "Built on a rock the Church shall stand, Even while steeples are falling."

Linda Sekela
Rummel, PA

Due to another commitment, our pastor at Lord of Life Lutheran, Garner, North Carolina, asked the lay assisting ministers to lead the congregation until he arrived. Just as we began singing an extra hymn, Pastor Joseph Tallent came down the aisle singing with us: "Here I Am, Lord."

Connie Fortmeyer
Garner, NC

"What do you mean, he's running late? I've spent three days adjusting her nap schedule around this baptism!"

License on a car belonging to Katie Adelman, choir director of Christ Lutheran Church in Bellevue, Washington, who wanted all to know "I do dee choir": **IDODQYR**.

Marianne Johnson
Chicago, IL

Say what?

One Sunday I received the message loud and clear that I need hearing aids. I thought I heard the pastor say: "We have some deaths this week," During the pause that followed I began to ponder who might have died when he continued, "Could they please stand up and identify themselves?"

Dale Goodman
Strawberry Point, IA

"Since you ran over an hour,
can we take it off of next week's service?"

Lutheran this and that

Readers of *Centre View*, a local newspaper in the northern Virginia suburbs of Washington, D.C., were startled by this headline:

"Holy Spirit Now Officially Lutheran." The story went on to discuss the organization of a new congregation, Holy Spirit Lutheran Church, Centreville, Virginia.

Paul M. Cross
Weirton, WV

I told my class of second- and third-graders at Bethlehem Lutheran Church, Cedar Falls, Iowa, that we are all saints. One boy, whose grandmother used to be Roman Catholic and is now Lutheran, broke in: "My grandma used to be a saint, but now she's a Lutheran."

Jody Streicher
Cedar Falls, IA

When the children at Community Lutheran Church, Las Vegas, Nevada, were asked on Reformation Sunday if they knew what day it was one little boy piped up, "It is Recommendation Sunday." Not a bad answer, we adults concluded.

Ruth Jette
Las Vegas, NV

Our pastor at Emmanuel Lutheran Church, High Point, North Carolina, asked the children, "Where do you think Martin Luther hung the 95 Theses?" My grandson, 5, who always raises his hand whether he knows the answer or not, said, "On a clothes line!"

Lois Harris
High Point, NC

I discussed with my young son the events of Holy Week, including Palm Sunday and how the events of the week led to Jesus' crucifixion and the crowds jeering him. I also explained how we, as Christians, all take part in Jesus' death. My son thought for a moment and said, "But Mom, we're not Christians. We're Lutherans."

Patty Chapman
Wadsworth, OH

I gave our daughter a rundown of the seven types of birdhouses scattered around our house, telling her the wrens are in the church birdhouse. She quipped, "So these must be Luth-wrens."

Adelheid Heyland
Boeme, TX

Our son, a student at the University of Iowa, Iowa City, went Christmas caroling with Lutheran Campus Ministry. At one nursing home he heard a woman say, "This is the third Lutheran church to come here. Don't any other churches sing?"

Karen Swanson
Dayton, IA

When my daughter, Emily, was trying my patience, I sent her to her room to think about how God wants us to be good Christians. Soon she appeared, crying and declaring, "I just don't know how you expect me to be a Christian, Mom. I'm Lutheran!"

Becky Soliss
New Braunfels, TX

Licensed to reform

Proud Lutheran Terry Eckard of Gastonia, North Carolina, sports this as his license plate: **MIT4TRES.**

Terry Eckard
Gastonia, NC

Lethargical renewal

Christ Lutheran Church in Marietta, Georgia, had just celebrated a joy-filled worship service in the style of a folk mass. A visitor from Hungary remarked, "It didn't seem like I was in the Lutheran church. I missed the lethargy."

Carolyn Baumgartner
Kennesaw, GA

I was watching *The Wizard of Oz* with friends and their children. When Auntie Em says to her crabby neighbor, "Elvira Gulch, for 23 years I've been dying to tell you what I've thought of you, but being a good Christian woman I can't say it," Aaron, 6, gave us a toothless smile and spouted, "I bet if she was Lutheran she'd tell her."

Lee Anne Gilson
Waldo, WI

"Church council is joining the going green
environmental movement and is recommending
that we serve only green jello at all potlucks."

Door-to-door Lutherans

When we received a chilly reception from one
man while distributing flyers door-to-door for
our Sunday school picnic I told my 7-year-old
daughter the man was likely gruff because
of another religious group noted for its
persistent door-to-door missionary work. My
daughter replied, "We'll, he was wrong. We're
not religious; we're Lutherans!"

Joyce Miller Bean
Chicago, IL

DAVE DRUMM

"We're not religious; we're Lutherans!"

As our daughter was preparing her Sunday
school lesson our granddaughter asked her
mother, "Jesus was Jewish?" "Yes," our
daughter answered. "Was Joseph Jewish?"
she asked. "Yes," was her mother's reply.
"Then Mary had to be the Lutheran in the
family!" our grandchild concluded.

Gertrude M. Smith
Columbia, SC

I asked for a volunteer to read the Bible
lesson while leading chapel for Charlotte
[North Carolina] Lutheran School. "What's
your name?" I asked. "Mark," the lad replied.
"Oh, you have the same name as our church,
St. Mark. Are you a saint?" The student
replied, "No, I'm not a saint. I'm a Lutheran."

C. Peter Setzer
Charlotte, NC

Through the seasons:
from Advent to Pentecost

© Jean Sorensen

**"Smile and pretend we're the family
in the Christmas letter I'm sending."**

Advent/Christmas

One Sunday in Advent, my prop for a children's sermon was an ultrasound picture of an 8-week-old fetus with a prominent umbilical cord. I compared how parents waiting for their unborn child are like people waiting for the Messiah—some things they know, some things they think they know and some things they won't know until the baby comes. To which one child chimed in, "One thing I know for sure is... it's a boy!"

Karen McNeill-Utecht
Lehigh Acres, FL

From *The Shepherd's Staff*, the newsletter of Good Shepherd Lutheran Church, Houghton, Michigan:

"Each Wednesday during Advent, the congregation will gather for prayer, medication and preparation. These informal services will be held in the lounge."

Armin Heidmann
LaCrosse, WI

I took my two sons to visit Santa last week. After the boys told him what they wanted, Santa pointed his finger at my 4-year-old, Jeff, and said, "Now be good, I'm watching you." Jeff asked, "You watch me all the time?" Santa replied, "Yes I do." Jeff said, "Well, then, you must know Jesus."

Jane Farmer
Decatur, IL

My 3-year-old son last Christmas said, "Mom, let's sing the door song." Puzzled, I asked him to sing a bit of it. He sang, "O Come let us adore him."

Shirley Robertson
Columbia, SC

During the Christmas season when many Lutheran churches were featuring lutefisk and lefse dinners, I decided to introduce this notion to our Argentinian exchange student. As we waited to be seated, a parishioner asked her if she liked fish. She readily replied, "Oh yes, I eat lots of fish in Argentina, but I have never eaten Lutheran fish."

Dorothy Hartman
Rochester, MN

"I've never eaten Lutheran fish."

A few years ago at Trinity Lutheran Church, Hicksville, New York, the midnight Christmas Eve service was so well-attended that late-arriving worshipers unfortunately had to be turned away at the door. The next Sunday many of those turned away placed their Christmas offering in the collection plate. On the back of an offering envelope, a member who was turned away wrote: "There was no room in the church so we went to the inn."

John H. Krahn
Levittown, NY

My 3-year-old granddaughter was helping me get the nativity figures ready to put out. When I handed her the first one, I said, "This is the Baby Jesus." She said, "We don't say Jesus. We say GOSH."

Phyllis Johnson
Reno, NV

Gregory, 3, was a shepherd for the outdoor living Nativity at Bethlehem Lutheran Church, Longmont, Colorado. When his mother asked if he'd like to participate next Christmas, Gregory said, "Yes. But next year I'd rather be a pirate."

Jonathan & Louanne Isernhagen
Longmont, CO

Our son and daughter-in-law have been foster parents for years, often dealing with caseworkers. When our grandchildren were deciding on parts to act out the Nativity, this was overheard from the playroom: "Oh, he can be Baby Jesus' caseworker."

Cynthia Merritt
Eugene, OR

From the Memorial Lutheran Church, St. Augustine, Florida, bulletin regarding the Christmas program:

"Special thanks to the choir and Sunday schoolers for special music and to Melissa G. for making the little beasts' costumes."

Doris Hubbell
St. Augustine, FL

The rash of Christmas specials on television had to have influenced our 8-year-old grand-daughter who during the opening hymn sang "Amazing grace, how sweet the sound, that saved a Grinch like me."

Michael L. Bennett
Massillon, OH

"Jesus was born in a manger,
not delivered by a stork like us."

Grace had a new baby sister and had learned some details about the birth experience. In Sunday school the teacher—looking for "wrapped him in swaddling clothes"—asked the 3-year-olds, "What did Mary do when Jesus was born?" But the class was stumped and silent. Finally Grace blurted out, "Mary had to push real hard!"

Al Bergh
Aurora, IL

When asked where the spirit of gift-giving at Christmas originated, my friend's 8-year-old said: "God gave us Jesus on Christmas." My friend was pleased with her answer, but after a short pause, the daughter added, "And Easter is when we sent him back!"

John LaMunyon
Sammamish, WA

My 5-year-old granddaughter, Amanda, told me on the phone that Christmas is to celebrate the birth of Jesus. I said, "It's so exciting. Are you going to bake him a cake?" She replied, "Naa, Mary will have to do it. Bethlehem's too far away."

Shirley Shakespeare
Towson, MD

Maggie, 3, and I were enjoying the holiday sights and sounds when she asked, "Mamma, what are you going to get me for Christmas?" I explained the true meaning of Christmas and how we do not think about what we get but rather what we give. A few thoughtful minutes later she asked, "What are you going to give me for Christmas?"

Dawn Gundlach
Riverview, FL

My grandson, Andrew, 3, struggled to put a towel up on the rack after his bath. After several unsuccessful attempts, it fell on his head. "Oh, well, I guess I'll just be a shepherd then," he said.

AnnaMarie DeYoung
Kyoto, Japan

When our 4-year-old grandson and 2-year-old granddaughter stayed with us in early December, we drove around looking at Christmas decorations and saw several Nativity scenes. We pointed out the different characters, including Baby Jesus in the manger. The next day Grandpa drove Ben to preschool on the same route we had taken the previous night. When Ben saw one of the Nativity scenes, he excitedly shouted, "Hey Grandpa—there's another one of those Jesus forts!"

Verna and Don Wallace
Mazomanie, WI

"If they were so smart, how come the wise men didn't bring Jesus a crib or at least a mattress?"

Epiphany

A few days after my niece's third birthday she and her cousin were playing with my Nativity set. My niece moved the pieces around, recounting the story as she remembered it—identifying the mommy and the daddy and the angels. Then she picked up the robed wise men carrying their urns and announced, "And then came the ladies with the coffee!"

Patricia Hemeleski
Bloomfield, NJ

I'm a preschool teacher. I asked my 4-year-olds, "What gifts did the wise men bring to baby Jesus?" One child answered, "Gold, frankincense and … maybe a shirt?"

Sandy Couser
Lima, OH

I asked a 4-year-old who was sporting a proud grin on his birthday if he had any goals for the year ahead. His mother laughed and said he didn't even know what goals were. "Yes I do," the lad replied. "That's what the wise men brought to the baby Jesus."

Marcia Garland
Columbia, PA

When visiting Appomattox Courthouse National Historical Park in Virginia, my husband pointed out to our grandson, Christopher, 5, the houses and then a stable on an area map, asking, "Do you know what you find in stables? Without missing a beat Christopher replied, "Babies."

Joanne Minich
Dover, DE

My daughter Janie, 5, repeated the Christmas story she'd learned at Sunday school. When asked what gifts the wise men brought she said, "Gold, myrrh and 50 cents."

Denise Gibson
Glenview, IL

The past year's Olympics have made their marks. A Sunday school class was asked, "What gifts did the wise men present to Jesus?" Someone did offer "Gold, frankincense and myrrh," but another girl asked, "Wasn't it gold, silver and bronze?"

Karl A. Schneider
Philadelphia, PA

Baptism of our Lord

The bulletin for Baptism of our Lord Sunday at Bethany Evangelical Lutheran Church, Burlington, Iowa, noted that "New members will be received by intinction."

Jackie Meyer
Burlington, IA

Ash Wednesday/Lent

During Lent I asked my Sunday school class at Holy Cross Lutheran Church, Excelsior, Minnesota, what they understood by "penance." After silence, one boy's face lit up as he answered, "That's what I've got hanging on my bedroom wall!"

William E. Oyler
Minnetonka, MN

Instructions for Ash Wednesday service at Good Shepherd Lutheran Church, Plover, Wisconsin:

"Those who desire to receive ashes come forward and keel at the rail."

Sue Marie Rendall
Almond, WI

I brought my neighbor to our Ash Wednesday service and explained to her the symbolism of the imposition of ashes. As they were applied to her forehead, the minister unintentionally said, "Remember that you are to dust." When we sat down my friend whispered to me, "She must have been in my house—she said, 'You are to dust.' "

Carolyn Fergus
Columbus, OH

"In no particular order, here is my list
of what you are giving up for Lent."

On Ash Wednesday I asked my 3-year-old son Eric where he would be going that afternoon. He said, "To church." I asked him if he knew what Pastor Hill would give him during the service. He replied, "Eyelashes."

Eric A. Kopp
Coram, NY

Holy Week

In the Palm Sunday bulletin at St. James Lutheran Church, Graniteville, South Carolina:

"The palm branches will be collected as you leave to be burned."

Ruth D. Orr
North Augusta, SC

I asked the confirmands the name of the garden where Jesus went to pray before he died. After a long pause, one ventured, "The Olive Garden?"

Julie Bergdahl
Plattsburgh, NY

During the children's sermon at St. Paul Lutheran Church, Pine Grove Mills, Pennsylvania, the pastor showed a Palm Sunday parade picture and asked why Jesus wasn't smiling. Most of the children looked puzzled, but one hand popped up: "He's sad," my son said, "because he knows it's going to rain."

Linda Rosensteel
Pennsylvania Furnace, PA

Our pastor was briefing the Trinity Lutheran Church, Flat Rock, Michigan, altar guild on general altar duties. The pastor explained the Maundy Thursday routine, "At the end of the evening service there is the ritual of Stripping the Altar Guild." Before he could retract his misstatement, a new guild member said, "Boy! What one has to do!"

Ida Henkel
Flat Rock, MI

During the Easter season, the pastor asked during the children's sermon: "What just happened to Jesus that we all want to remember?" After some thought, one of the children said, "Jesus died on the cross." Pressing on, the pastor asked, "And what did God do then?" The pastor's son spoke right up, "God recycled him!"

Terry L. Daly
Warren, MI

"This year instead of Easter eggs, you'll be
hunting for my sunglasses, checkbook,
and the green bracelet Grandma gave me."

Easter

My 5-year-old granddaughter who attends Calvary Lutheran Church, Seneca Falls, New York, was overwhelmed by the large attendance on Easter. She whispered to her mother, "Are some of these people in the wrong church?"

Mildred T. Ludwig
Seaford, NY

We attended Easter worship with our son and his family in Pennsylvania. Our son handed his 5-year-old son his offering, but he looked down the pew and saw his grandfather holding his money. He looked up at his dad and said, "That's OK. Grandpa's buying."

Carol H. Hultine
Princeton, IL

"How come Easter is the only time
God cares about what we wear?"

© Jean Sorensen

"Pentecost is my favorite
church holiday—no crowds."

Pentecost

The Evangelical Lutheran Church, Babbit, Minnesota, church bulletin asked members:

"Bring a red geranium plant to church next Sunday. It will make the chancel festive for Pentecost... Also, you might consider wearing something next Sunday in celebration of Pentecost."

Corrine Olsen
Babbit, MN

Good answers

**"That for which you are so eager to be
thankful will be another half hour."**

Our pastor was introducing new members to the congregation, asking each in turn, "What do you do?" "Are you a homemaker?" "Where do you work?" With a smile on his face, one honest little boy said, "I make a mess!"

Laila M. Whitfield
Marquette, MI

Megan, our 4-year-old granddaughter, attends Our Savior Lutheran Church preschool in Livermore, California. Holy Week she came home from school and announced, "Jesus died on the cross. But he's getting better now, and he'll be all right by Sunday."

Eloise Straight
Livermore, CA

Our pastor at Christ Lutheran Church, Long Beach, California, was telling the story of the wedding at Cana. After he told how Jesus turned water into wine, he asked if anyone knew what that was called. Without hesitation, one little charmer blurted out: "Recycling."

Margaret Madsen
Anaheim, CA

During "Kid Talk" at St. John Lutheran Church, Glendale, Arizona, the pastor asked about the types of angels and their jobs. Having already talked about herald and warrior angels, he was trying to get them to identify archangels. He asked, "What do you suppose archangels do?" Laura, 9, confidently answered, "Ride along with Noah."

Jaye Thompson
Glendale, AZ

I was getting accurate answers as I asked the children about Old Testament stories we'd studied: "Samson was ...?" "A judge!" "David was ...?" "A king!" To "Jeremiah was ...?" a quick-witted fifth-grader offered: "A bullfrog!"

Joel Rova Hegener
Silverdale, WA

In the children's talk at Hope Lutheran church, El Sobrante, California, Pastor Mark Gruebmeyer asked, "What do you think it's like in heaven?" A boy answered, "Cloudy."

Doris Graesser
El Sobrante, CA

In a children's sermon focusing on the call of Jesus' first disciples, I asked: "If you were fishing for people, what kind of bait would you use?" I believe young Cole was onto something when he suggested, "Chocolate!"

Elizabeth Jaeger
Sheboygan Falls, WI

What's so funny about weddings and funerals? Plenty!

© Jean Sorensen

"We'd like a church wedding, but take it easy on the religious overtones."

The young pastor, now a Lutheran chaplain in South Dakota, was beaming, as were the bride and groom before him. All had gone well with his first wedding. In waiting for the recessional to begin, he leaned over to ask the bride if she wanted to kiss. With that, she leaned over the altar rail, gave the pastor a kiss, then took the groom by the arm and marched out—leaving a very red-faced pastor behind.

David J. Webster
Porter, MN

When the pastor at Crow River Lutheran Church, Belgrade, Minnesota, asked his confirmands to give a Bible verse pertaining to marriage, one young man quickly responded, "Father, forgive them for they know not what they do."

Ann Haugen
New London, MN

Too much joy

At their wedding, my friends chose to have the congregation sing the majestic hymn, "Joyful, Joyful We Adore Thee." Verses were printed in the worship folder, but the third line down clearly read, "Melt the clouds of sin and sadness, Drive the groom of doubt away...."

Kristin Zemmol
Buena Park, CA

Clergy fired

The groom was tall—so tall I had to lift the cup to him when serving him and his bride communion. I missed my mark and the red wine dribbled down the front of his white shirt and tuxedo. With good humor he looked me in the eye and deadpanned, "You're fired."

William Kees
Park Ridge, IL

"Exactly how hard would it be to make the stained glass match my wedding colors?"

When I was serving a Minnesota parish, an elderly member went to spend her final years with a daughter in Oregon. When she died, a funeral director arranged to send her cremains to Minnesota for the funeral and burial. On the day of the funeral the cremains had not arrived. When the local funeral director checked it out, he learned that her ashes were accidentally sent to another state and wouldn't arrive until the following day. With fear and trepidation he told the woman's two daughters the bad news. "That's OK," responded one of the daughters, "Mother always loved to travel."

Roger Buhr
Decorah, IA

My friend Cathy's husband, Tom, died several years ago and was cremated. Following his memorial service, Cathy and her immediate family went home. Cathy had a feeling she'd forgotten something when it hit her: the urn! She told me she could just hear Tom, who had a dry sense of humor, saying, "Gone *and* forgotten...."

Joann Abrahamsen
Yonkers, NY

The funeral director gathered family and friends around the grave site. He went over to the hearse, looked for the electronic "clicker" key and realized it was on the front seat. The hearse had automatically locked and he had to announce that the deceased was locked inside (until another key could be found). The deceased was quite a prankster, and we all agreed this was his last, best prank ever—avoiding the grave.

David S. Schafer
Westminster, MD

Stewardship
and other money matters

"And to my nephew, who never put anything in the collection plate, I leave his share of the inheritance to the church."

My daughter, her husband and their 6-year-old son, Jon, came with me to church at First Lutheran, Johnstown, Pennsylvania, recently. When the collection plate was passed, Jon's father gave him a quarter. Jon noticed his father and mother each gave a dollar. Coming out of church, Jon said, "Now I get it. It's a quarter for kids and a dollar for grown-ups!"

Katherine Abele
Johnstown, PA

Recession cession

A member of our pastors' study group had a great idea for church-state relations in these recessionary times. He quipped, "The greatest thing the federal government could do for the church is to stop printing $1 bills."

Julie A. Hart
Belleville, IL

During my sermon an older woman fainted and struck her head on a pew. As an ambulance crew wheeled her out on a stretcher she motioned for her daughter, who thought she might be summoning strength to convey her final words. Instead, Mary whispered into her daughter's ear, "My offering is in my purse." This devoted steward made a full recovery.

Eric Hulstrand
Portland, ND

The pastor, demonstrating tithing, had 10 bowls carried to the front, each containing 10 food items. He placed the first item on a table saying, "One for the Lord" and the other nine items on another table "for us." When he came to the bowl of 10 bananas, he asked, "Now who gets the first banana?" A little boy with a big voice shouted, "The monkey!"

James Lieberknecht
Thousand Oaks, CA

For the children's sermon on stewardship Sunday, my husband counted out, one by one, nine of 10 dollar bills into a child's hand. Then he held up the remaining bill and asked, "Is this too much to give back to God?" With deafening conviction a little boy shouted, "Yes!" My husband seized the moment to drive home the point: "It seems some of your parents think the same way."

Betty Ulrich
Stone Lake, WI

The Old Testament text was from Jeremiah, so I asked the kids, "Can anyone tell me what a prophet is?" A boy answered, "Oh yes, it's when you have a lemonade stand, and you pay back your mom for the ingredients, and what's left is your profit."

Margie P. Fiedler
Spokane, WA

Congregational life

© David W. Harbaugh

"In order to develop a closer relationship with my congregation, I'll be leading the worship service from a different pew every Sunday."

Recently I ordered from amazon.com some books for our church, Christ the King Lutheran, South Bend, Indiana. The next time I used my church computer to visit the web site, I received the following greeting, "Hello, Christ... If you are not Christ click here."

Maretta Hershberger
South Bend, IN

Sam, the sound technician, neglected to activate the lectern microphone at Mount Calvary Lutheran Church, Cypress, California, when the Bible school chair went to make an announcement. She drew smiles from the congregation when she called to him, "Turn me on, Sam." Sam is her husband.

Mitzi Bartlett
Garden Grove, CA

The secretary at United Lutheran Church, Manteca, California, was calling parishioners to find readers for a Lenten lesson. She told one man, "You have the smallest part—God."

Deborah J. Grochau
Manteca, CA

When it was announced at church that the purchase of the adjacent laundromat had been completed, my husband leaned over and whispered, "Now cleanliness *is* next to godliness."

Carol Savolaine
Westerville, OH

When *The Lutheran* makes the "Light side"

"She's legendary! Her bulletin bloopers have made no less than eight *Lutheran* 'Light sides.'"

Recycling guidelines in the *Decorah* [Iowa] *Journal*:

"Only extremely slick magazines and catalogs will be accepted. Other magazines with dull pages, such as *TV Guide*, *Reader's Digest* and *The Lutheran* should be placed with newspaper recycling in bins around the county."

J. Martin-Schramm
New York, NY

Annoyed by the persistent buzzing of a fly in her office at Augustana Lutheran Church, Denver, the publications manager strode into the main office and asked, "Do we have any old *Lutherans* I can use to swat flies with?"

Lyn Washburn
Denver, CO

In the St. Paul Lutheran Church, Burnham, Pennsylvania, bulletin:

"Balony Class—the Balcony Sunday school class is beginning a new unit using a series of articles reprinted from *The Lutheran*."

D.W. Beaver
Burnham, PA

Gotcha 'Lutheran'

As a church secretary, I can't resist tossing this one back at *The Lutheran*. In the wedding ideas column (February 2004, page 38), one of the ceremonies featured "signers for the visually impaired." Huh?

Nancy Olson
Taylor, WI

© Ed Fischer

I asked the first year confirmation class at Mauldin, South Carolina, "Who is Martin Luther?" A teenage boy replied eagerly, "He was the guy who invented *The Lutheran*."

Rodney W. Parrott
Charleston, SC

Study Guide

The humor (and occasional profundity) found on these pages can also be used in a group—for adult education or small groups. Use the stories and cartoons as jumping off points to discuss church life and faith issues, and how the gift of humor sustains you.

Think back

Share with one other person or group:

- What comic strip/book or cartoon did you grow up reading? What messages did you get from it?
- What cartoons or comics do you read today?
- What are the elements of a good cartoon or comic? Why do people like them so much?
- When you think of humor and the church, what experiences or people come to mind?

Master cartoonist

Charles Schulz, who was reared in the Lutheran faith, was renowned for mixing humor and religion in *Peanuts*. He even said Linus represented his spiritual side. In later years, Schulz said his philosophical views had changed over the years. Still, he was driven by a belief in the obligation humans have for one another and the world.

- What *Peanuts* character represents your spiritual side?
- How has your faith or life philosophy changed over the years?
- How has a sense of humor shaped your faith and/or religious views?

Kids say the wisest...

Most of the submissions to the "Light side" are stories about, or quotes from, children. Page through the chapter "Kids say the wisest things" and share with one another one or more of your favorites.

- What is it about children that makes their life observations
    so profound?
- What lesson have you learned from a child in your life?
- How do you keep your own faith child-like?

Scripture laugh

Sarah, wife of Abraham, is famous for laughing in the Bible (Genesis 18). Childless in her later years, she laughs when overhearing an angel tell Abraham she will bear a child. The laughter—and her denying it—earn Sarah a divine "tsk tsk." Later Sarah names her son Isaac (Hebrew for laughter). The Bible is clear that the first cousins of humor—cheerfulness, joy and gladness—abound:

- "A cheerful heart is a good medicine, but a downcast spirit
    dries up the bones." (Proverbs 17:22)
- "Then our mouth was willed with laughter, and our tongue with
    shouts of joy..." (Psalm 126:2)
- "Worship the Lord with gladness..." (Psalm 100:2a)

Search for, and share with one another, stories of laughter, cheerfulness, joy and gladness found in the scriptures. Close with prayer, thanking God for the gift of humor, for those who have brought humor to our lives, and for the hope that humor and people stir within us.